It's a
Boy

summersdale

IT'S A BOY

An Hachette UK Company
www.hachette.co.uk

Summersdale Publishers Ltd
Part of Octopus Publishing Group Limited
Carmelite House
50 Victoria Embankment
LONDON
EC4Y 0DZ
UK

www.summersdale.com

Printed and bound in China

ISBN: 978-1-78685-789-7

Substantial discounts on bulk quantities of Summersdale books are available to corporations, professional associations and other organisations. For details contact general enquiries: telephone: +44 (0) 1243 771107 or email: enquiries@summersdale.com.

A GRAND
ADVENTURE
IS ABOUT
TO BEGIN.

A. A. MILNE

If you're interested in finding out more about our books, find us on Facebook at Summersdale Publishers and follow us on Twitter at @Summersdale.

www.summersdale.com

To ....

From ....

A new baby is like
the beginning of all
things — wonder,
hope, a dream
of possibilities.

EDA J. LESHAN

Babies are such a nice
way to start people.

DON HEROLD

NO ANIMAL
IS SO
INEXHAUSTIBLE
AS AN
EXCITED
INFANT.

AMY LESLIE

A person's a person, no matter how small!

DR SEUSS

If I have a
monument in this
world, it is my son.

MAYA ANGELOU

**People who say
they sleep like a
baby usually don't
have one.**

LEO BURKE

BABIES ARE
ALWAYS
MORE
TROUBLE
THAN YOU
THOUGHT –
AND MORE
WONDERFUL.

CHARLES OSGOOD

It's extraordinary to
look into a baby's face and
see a piece of your flesh
and your spirit.

LIAM NEESON

With boys,
you always know
where you stand.
Right in the path
of a hurricane.

ERMA BOMBECK

Always... be a little
kinder than necessary.

J. M. BARRIE

The raising of a child is the building of a cathedral. You can't cut corners.

DAVE EGGERS

Love crawls with the baby,
walks with the toddler,
runs with the child, then
stands aside to let the
youth walk into adulthood.

JO ANN MERRELL

Do all things with love.

OG MANDINO

Have children while
your parents
are still young
enough to take
care of them.

RITA RUDNER

Boys are found everywhere
– on top of, underneath,
inside of, climbing on,
swinging from, running
around or jumping to.

ALAN MARSHALL BECK

What is a home without children? Quiet.

HENNY YOUNGMAN

A baby is sunshine and
moonbeams and more,
brightening your world
as never before.

ANONYMOUS

The only man who
has stolen my heart
is my son.

SANDRA BULLOCK

EVERYTHING
IN OUR LIFE
SHOULD BE
BASED
ON LOVE.

RAY BRADBURY

You can't understand it until you experience the simple joy of the first time your son points at a seagull and says 'duck'.

RUSSELL CROWE

We never know
the love of a parent
till we become
parents ourselves.

HENRY WARD BEECHER

We find a delight in the beauty and happiness of children that makes the heart too big for the body.

RALPH WALDO EMERSON

If your children look
up to you, you've made a
success of life's biggest job.

I hope I can be as good of a father to my son as my dad was to me.

CALVIN JOHNSON

If you want
your children
to listen, try
talking softly –
to someone else.

ANN LANDERS

WRINKLES
ARE
HEREDITARY
– PARENTS
GET THEM
FROM THEIR
CHILDREN.

DORIS DAY

The quickest way
for a parent to get
a child's attention
is to sit down and
look comfortable.

LANE OLINGHOUSE

Even when freshly
washed and relieved of
all obvious confections,
children tend to be sticky.

FRAN LEBOWITZ

I LOVE WHEN I TEACH MY SON A GOOD LESSON. BUT I LOVE IT EVEN MORE WHEN HE TEACHES ME.

BRAD MELTZER

I do not love
him because he is
good, but because
he is my child.

Each day of our
lives we make deposits
in the memory banks
of our children.

CHARLES R. SWINDOLL

Children see magic because they look for it.

CHRISTOPHER MOORE

OUR
GREATEST
NATURAL
RESOURCE
IS THE
MINDS
OF OUR
CHILDREN.

WALT DISNEY

Setting a good example
for your children takes all
the fun out of middle age.

WILLIAM FEATHER

Before I got married I had six theories about bringing up children; now I have six children and no theories.

JOHN WILMOT

Children reinvent
your world for you.

SUSAN SARANDON

When you become
a parent, it is your
biggest chance to
grow again. You
have another crack
at yourself.

FRED ROGERS

We worry about what
a child will be tomorrow,
yet we forget he is
someone today.

STACIA TAUSCHER

A child is not a
vase to be filled,
but a fire to be lit.

FRANÇOIS RABELAIS

There is nothing like a newborn baby to renew your spirit and to buttress your resolve to make the world a better place.

VIRGINIA KELLEY

Having an infant son
alerts me to the fact that
every man, at one point,
has peed on his own face.

OLIVIA WILDE

The essential
skill of parenting is
making up answers.

DAVE BARRY

To witness the birth
of a child is our best
opportunity to experience
the meaning of the
word 'miracle'.

PAUL CARVEL

The soul is healed by
being with children.

FYODOR DOSTOEVSKY

A BABY IS
THE MOST
COMPLICATED
OBJECT MADE
BY UNSKILLED
LABOUR.

ANONYMOUS

Loving a baby is a circular business... the more you give the more you get.

PENELOPE LEACH

**A boy's story is the
best that is ever told.**

CHARLES DICKENS

Act as if what
you do makes
a difference.
It does.

WILLIAM JAMES

Parents learn a lot
from their children
about coping with life.

MURIEL SPARK

I understood once
I held a baby in my
arms, why some people
have the need to keep
having them.

SPALDING GRAY

Your children need your presence more than your presents.

JESSE JACKSON

A PERSON
SOON LEARNS
HOW LITTLE
HE KNOWS
WHEN A
CHILD BEGINS
TO ASK
QUESTIONS.

RICHARD L. EVANS

Birth is an experience that demonstrates that life is not merely function and utility, but form and beauty.

CHRISTOPHER LARGEN

A fairly bright boy is
far more intelligent and
far better company than
the average adult.

J. B. S. HALDANE

LIFE DOESN'T
COME
WITH AN
INSTRUCTION
BOOK;
THAT'S WHY
WE HAVE
PARENTS.

ANONYMOUS

When I grow up
I want to be a
little boy.

JOSEPH HELLER

You can learn many
things from children.
How much patience
you have, for instance.

FRANKLIN P. JONES

Children must be taught how to think, not what to think.

MARGARET MEAD

A BABY IS
BORN WITH
A NEED TO
BE LOVED –
AND NEVER
OUTGROWS IT.

FRANK A. CLARK

The hand that rocks the cradle is usually attached to someone who isn't getting enough sleep.

JOHN FIEBIG

A small son
can charm himself
into, and out of,
most things.

JENNY DE VRIES

Words cannot express
the joy of new life.

HERMANN HESSE

A parent is someone
who carries pictures in
their wallet where their
money used to be.

ANONYMOUS

To the world you
may be one person;
but to one person you
may be the world.

DR SEUSS

You will always
be your child's
favourite toy.

VICKI LANSKY

Children use all their wiles to get their way with adults. Adults do the same with children.

MASON COOLEY

Children are the world's
most valuable resource and
its best hope for the future.

JOHN F. KENNEDY

Love for children is perhaps the most intense love.

WERNER BERGENGRUEN

Sometimes… the smallest
things take up the most
room in your heart.

A. A. MILNE

It's the merry-hearted
boys that make the
best men!

IRISH PROVERB

EVERY
CHILD IS
ONE CARING
ADULT AWAY
FROM BEING
A SUCCESS
STORY.

JOSH SHIPP

Whether your child is 3 or 13, don't rush in to rescue him until you know he's done all he can to rescue himself.

BARBARA F. MELTZ

Every baby needs a lap.

HENRY ROBIN

My heart is now
outside my body.

CHRISSY TEIGEN

Sons are the anchors
of a mother's life.

SOPHOCLES

It's a very powerful
feeling to see the
product of your
love right there
in front of you.

JOHN LEGEND

It is the nature
of babies to
be in bliss.

DEEPAK CHOPRA

MY NUMBER
ONE GOAL
IS TO LOVE,
SUPPORT
AND BE
THERE FOR
MY SON.

FARRAH FAWCETT

All that children need is love, a grown-up to take responsibility for them, and a soft place to land.

DEBORAH HARKNESS

Having a baby
dragged me, kicking
and screaming, from the
world of self-absorption.

PAUL REISER

MY NEW
FAVOURITE
SMELL IS
NEW BABY
SMELL. IT
MAKES ME
SO HAPPY.

JANE KRAKOWSKI

It takes courage
to raise children.

JOHN STEINBECK

A baby will make love stronger, days shorter, nights longer, bankroll smaller, home happier, clothes shabbier, the past forgotten, and the future worth living for.

ANONYMOUS

A child is an uncut diamond.

AUSTIN O'MALLEY

ALL MY
EGGS ARE IN
ONE BASKET,
AND THAT'S
MY FAMILY.

BLAKE LIVELY

No other stranger cares
that your kid ate an
artichoke, but you think
it's the best story ever.

JIMMY FALLON

Having a baby
is a life-changer.
It gives you a whole
other perspective on
why you wake up
every day.

TAYLOR HANSON

Children make you want
to start life over.

MUHAMMAD ALI

I wanted to call
my parents and say,
'I'm sorry, because I
never knew how much
you loved me.'

ASHTON KUTCHER

If it's an oak tree, I want
it to grow as an oak tree.
I'm not going to try to
force it to be an apple tree.

WILL SMITH

The most important mark I will leave on this world is my son.

SARAH SHAHI

He was born with a
gift of laughter.

RAFAEL SABATINI

Children have neither
past nor future. They
enjoy the present, which
very few of us do.

JEAN DE LA BRUYÈRE

Once you bring kids into the world, it's not about you any more.

TONY GASKINS

Your greatest contribution
may not be something you
do but someone you raise.

ANONYMOUS

The first happiness
of a child is to know
that he is loved.

DON BOSCO

LITTLE BOYS
DON'T TAKE
BATHS –
THEY JUST
DUST OFF.

ANONYMOUS

If you want your children to turn out well, spend twice as much time with them and half as much money.

ABIGAIL VAN BUREN

Where there is great love, there are always miracles.

WILLA CATHER

There is no friendship,
no love, like that of the
parent for the child.

HENRY WARD BEECHER

When you hold an
infant, hold him not just
with your body, but with
your mind and heart.

MAGDA GERBER

Boys are beyond the range of anybody's sure understanding, at least when they are between the ages of 18 months and 90 years.

JAMES THURBER

Children are a
bridge to heaven.

PERSIAN PROVERB

EVERY BABY
BORN INTO
THE WORLD
IS A FINER
ONE THAN
THE LAST.

CHARLES DICKENS

You hear people say it all the time, how life changes so drastically. But you can't possibly grasp how beautiful that is until you have your child.

PINK

A boy is a magical
creature. You can lock
him out of your workshop,
but you can't lock him
out of your heart.

ALAN MARSHALL BECK

A PERFECT
EXAMPLE OF
MINORITY
RULE IS A
BABY IN
THE HOUSE.

ANONYMOUS

Kids go
where there
is excitement.
They stay where
there is love.

ZIG ZIGLAR

What good mothers and
fathers instinctively
feel like doing for their
babies is usually
best after all.

BENJAMIN SPOCK

The child must know
that he is a miracle.

PABLO CASALS

I'M SO
PROUD OF
YOU THAT
IT MAKES
ME PROUD
OF ME.

JOHN GREEN

There is no way
to be a perfect parent,
and a million ways
to be a good one.

ANONYMOUS

You aren't wealthy
until you have
something money
can't buy.

GARTH BROOKS

Every child begins
the world again.

HENRY DAVID THOREAU

There is absolutely
no way that labour
is harder than
installing a car seat.

CHRISSY TEIGEN

Wherever you go,
go with all
your heart.

CONFUCIUS

If my son is
happy, then
I am happy.

CHRIS PAUL

While we try to teach our children all about life, our children teach us what life is all about.

ANONYMOUS

If I were ever under attack, I would use my wife as a human shield to protect that baby.

RYAN REYNOLDS

I didn't expect
babies to need so
many diapers.

SHAKIRA

We cannot always build
the future for our youth,
but we can build our
youth for the future.

FRANKLIN D. ROOSEVELT

Hugs can do great
amounts of good –
especially for children.

PRINCESS DIANA

MY MOTHER
HAD A
GREAT DEAL
OF TROUBLE
WITH ME,
BUT I
THINK SHE
ENJOYED IT.

MARK TWAIN

You know you're
in love when you
can't fall asleep
because reality is
finally better than
your dreams.

ANONYMOUS

**In time of test,
family is best.**

BURMESE PROVERB

There was never a child so lovely but his mother was glad to get him to sleep.

RALPH WALDO EMERSON

Think of stretch marks as
pregnancy service stripes.

JOYCE ARMOR

The best and most
beautiful things in the
world cannot be seen or
even touched. They must
be felt with the heart.

HELEN KELLER

Every beetle is a
gazelle in the eyes
of its mother.

MOORISH PROVERB

MAY YOU
LIVE EVERY
DAY OF
YOUR LIFE.

JONATHAN SWIFT

Children will not remember you for the material things you provided, but for the feeling that you cherished them.

RICHARD L. EVANS

Getting a burp out of your little thing is probably the greatest satisfaction I've come across.

BRAD PITT

IN THE
GARDEN OF
HUMANITY
EVERY
BABY IS A
FRESH NEW
FLOWER.

DEBASISH MRIDHA

Children learn
to smile from
their parents.

SHINICHI SUZUKI

A baby is something
you carry inside you
for nine months, in
your arms for three
years and in your heart
till the day you die.

MARY MASON

Families are like fudge – mostly sweet with a few nuts.

ANONYMOUS

DON'T LIMIT
A CHILD TO
YOUR OWN
LEARNING,
FOR HE WAS
BORN IN
ANOTHER
TIME.

RABINDRANATH TAGORE

There are only two lasting
bequests we can hope to
give our children. One is
roots. The other is wings.

HODDING CARTER

A boy becomes an adult three years before his parents think he does, and about two years after he thinks he does.

LEWIS B. HERSHEY

A boy's will is
the wind's will.

HENRY WADSWORTH
LONGFELLOW

Boys do not grow up gradually. They move forward in spurts like the hands of clocks in railway stations.

CYRIL CONNOLLY

Children are a
great comfort in your
old age – and they help
you reach it faster, too.

ANONYMOUS

Children
make your life
important.

ERMA BOMBECK

I love to think that the day you're born, you're given the world as your birthday present.

LEO BUSCAGLIA

Raising kids is part joy
and part guerrilla warfare.

ED ASNER

The rules for
parents are three...
love, limit, and
let them be.

ELAINE M. WARD

She loved a little boy very,
very much – even more
than she loved herself.

SHEL SILVERSTEIN

Everything depends
on upbringing.

LEO TOLSTOY

YOU HAVE A LIFETIME TO WORK, BUT CHILDREN ARE ONLY YOUNG ONCE.

POLISH PROVERB

Don't ever tell
the mother of
a newborn that
her baby's smile
is just gas.

ANONYMOUS

His laughter...
sparkled like a splash
of water in sunlight.

JOSEPH LELYVELD

When you are dealing
with a child, keep all
your wits about you,
and sit on the floor.

AUSTIN O'MALLEY

There's no road map
on how to raise a
family: it's always an
enormous negotiation.

MERYL STREEP

Always kiss your children goodnight, even if they're already asleep.

H. JACKSON BROWN JR

Family is not an important thing. It's everything.

MICHAEL J. FOX